The American Poetry Review/Honickman
First Book Prize

THE HONICKMAN FOUNDATION is dedicated to the support of projects that promote spiritual growth and creativity, education and social change. At the heart of the mission of the Honickman Foundation is the belief that creativity enriches contemporary society because the arts are powerful tools for enlightenment, equity and empowerment, and must be encouraged to effect social change as well as personal growth. A current focus is on the particular power of photography and poetry to reflect and interpret reality, and, hence, to illuminate all that is true.

The annual American Poetry Review/Honickman First Book Prize offers publication of a book of poems, a $3,000 award, distribution by Copper Canyon Press through Consortium, and a $1,000 grant for a book tour.

Each year a distinguished poet is chosen to judge the prize and write an introduction to the winning book. The purpose of the prize is to encourage excellence in poetry, and to provide a wide readership for a deserving first book of poems. *Ivory Cradle* is the third book in the series.

**Winners of
The American Poetry Review/Honickman
First Book Prize**

Joshua Beckman, *Things Are Happening*   1998

Dana Levin, *In the Surgical Theatre*   1999

Anne Marie Macari, *Ivory Cradle*   2000

Ivory Cradle

Ivory Cradle

poems by

Anne Marie Macari

WINNER OF THE APR / HONICKMAN
FIRST BOOK PRIZE

THE AMERICAN POETRY REVIEW
PHILADELPHIA

Direct all inquiries to
The APR/Honickman First Book Prize
The American Poetry Review
1721 Walnut Street
Philadelphia, PA 19103

Distribution by Copper Canyon Press/Consortium

Library of Congress Catalogue Card Number: 00-131696

ISBN 978-0-9663395-6-7

First edition

Thanks to the editors of the following magazines,
where some of the poems in this book first appeared:
The Cortland Review: Glory;
The Cream City Review: American Music;
Field: Clare And Francis; Dialogue: 14th Century; Clare Views
the Body of Francis; The Woods Behind the House;
Poetry Northwest: Vermont Trees;
The Ohio Review: My Son and I See the Arms and Armor Exhibit;
Triquarterly: Between Heaven and Earth

The author wishes to express her gratitude to Robert Creeley.
Also to Joan Larkin and Thomas Lux; and to Gerald Stern
for his endless support.

Contents

PART TWO

For Jerry
and for Noah, Lukas, and Jeremy

Introduction

BY ROBERT CREELEY

NOW AND AGAIN one comes upon a story so quietly and articulately told that it stays in mind long after, echoing, recasting the usual frames of reference and order, making whatever it is the world had been thought to be quite changed and even, again, unknown. Perhaps any presence thus insistent of someone else's 'real life,' as they say, has this effect, brings one out of the securing habits of one's own daily location and purpose. Yet such displacement as I note has little to do with great events of a usual kind. There are no vast, enclosing wars, no isolating heights of human endeavor. In contrast this book is a quiet if intense place, a proposal of such genuine modesty and hope one is moved by that fact alone, however much else there is of a remarkable authority.

A poem of Robert Graves, "To Juan at the Winter Solstice," begins with a conviction it's taken centuries to recognize, much less to alter. "There is one story, and one story only, that is worth your telling . . ." That story, of course, is of the King's "starry rise and starry fall," the cycle of the seasons, the ritual order of our common world, invested as male avatar and continuity. The woman, so to speak, is the responsive or denying presence of that world itself, the physical, the fated.

She is, in Graves's emphasis—and it is a brilliantly sustained one—the traditional White Goddess. But what then of women themselves? How shall they relate to this "one story," and is it theirs too?

I felt these questions becoming insistent as I first read this singular work. For one thing, these *were* truly stories and the rituals implicit in them shared place with the acts I witnessed in reading. Then there were seemingly many of them, although I slowly recognized that, even as in Graves's proposition, here as well there was "one only." The story of the family, the story of the witnessing and testifying woman of this family, the story of the place they had come from, the story of the traditions of that place, which secured it in history, the story of the children, sons, of a father rejecting, of a friend's death, of—at one consummate moment—a voice saying:

That's how you rise now from your chair,

rise to your grief, your shining eyes on me,
your hand pressing mine so I'm stunned by what I'm losing,

what I've lost, stunned by how we go on, still loving
and loved, standing here, consumed by light.

This comes from another side of our human story, comes, in Robert Duncan's phrase, "from a well deeper than time . . . " The story of Saint Clare and Saint Francis underlies it—provokes it: "But it was Francis who kept her here, ordering her to eat/ a bit of bread each day,/ to keep the taste of the world/ on her tongue. I go back to this story over and over." As must we all—and what of that curious obligation to so stay, to sustain the belief by our faith, to put from us all that would argue our own determining will, insisting we maintain a thread passing so fragilely through our fingers? This trial would seem to be that which belief itself must survive.

Keeping the faith is a daily act, having nothing to do with containment, with securing knowledge, even with those precedents that might appear to aid its extraordinarily lonely undertaking. *I acted in blind faith,* one says—and yet others must of necessity be related, acknowledged. These are not only the echoing stories of a church's sanctified persons. The wonders here are those of perception, intuition, union, separation —and all the emotions these provoke. Anger, despair, but also joy, love in its flooding recognitions, relief in the world's insistent substance.

What shall one do with outrage, with a displacement so complete that it leaves no ground at all but the body's, nothing left? Were there some heroic size finally to be gained, some scale of possibility faint but implicit, these poems would be all too familiar, and the lives they follow in the proposal of their own—sons and saints equally—would soon fade altogether. It is, rather, that there is no relief, no solution or ending to be come to. Only *place* itself can offer a place to be, a chance to recognize the world with whatever one has brought to it. Sounds, odors, rain, sky, dirt, arms, legs, all specific—and without a distance or enclosing meaning.

Here at the edge of an imagined time—not at all that of this consummate poet but of our own indulgent prospect—I think of Wordsworth's writing 200 years ago:

A slumber did my spirit seal;
   I had no human fears:
She seemed a thing that could not feel
   The touch of earthly years.

No motion has she now, no force;
   She neither hears nor sees;
Rolled round in earth's diurnal course,
   With rocks, and stones, and trees.

(1799)

It's as if, then, the collective thought of the two centuries following had been most intently addressed to that displacing recognition. Time, despite it is a human invention, still sits within boundaries one can neither anticipate nor change. Why is the world so indifferent and ourselves perhaps the best instance of that fact? "But why the torture," as W. C. Williams wrote, the brutality, the waste of such time as one's been given—if there was ever something to be saved?

Reading these poems again in the past weeks, I must make clear that they have taken me far beyond their simply apparent mastery. Years ago Pound emphasized, "Only emotion endures," saying, "Nothing counts save the quality of the affection." Another friend noted that my generation gave extraordinary authority to feeling, seeming, he said, to make it take precedence over all else that might happen in a poem. So Denise Levertov writes, "If we're going to be here, let's be here now. . . . " The shatter and dislocation of our common world, its bitter habits of authority, the persistent loss of identifying place, all that one recalls now as "existentialism," made the singular fact of "person" loom with an extraordinary scale upon the surface of that earth we had so presumed to know.

> The sky was full like the sea
> of wandering phosphorous that came
> with its old forgotten lives and swelled
> closer though we hardly looked
> and when we did it was the ivory cradle,
> polished and rocking—so empty
> over the trees—that caught our eyes
> because it belonged to us, and I,
> who never had the patience to find
> patterns in the stars but only stood
> helpless, my feet digging in cold sand,

waiting, listening to the surf
rise and fall, lay down with you
for a better view, though no tunnel
opened up, no vision completed us,
even for a moment. But we were happy,
your hand with its heat and bones
just so around mine while we watched
the flowering dark

(from "Ivory Cradle")

Here is a world beyond our intention, understanding or acceptance, and we arrive there, it seems, because it is where we always were, no matter. There is no other reason and there never was. That firmament upon which we project our hopeful identifications and recognitions can only be "so empty/ over the trees . . ." Yet, significantly, it endures as a presence, a place we humanly come to—not heaven but "flowering dark"—through all imagined time and space. *Praesepe** (which in Latin means "Cradle" or "Manger") is also called "Beehive"—another initiatory *place* of these poems. It is a cluster of several hundred stars in the zodiacal constellation Cancer. "Visible to the unaided eye as a small patch of bright haze, it was first distinguished as a group of stars by Galileo. It was included by Hipparchus in the earliest known star catalog, c. 129 B.C." *Praesepe*, as the Encyclopaedia Britannica notes, was used even before Hipparchus' time. "The name Beehive is of uncertain but more recent origin."

One so longs for an annealing system, for meaning's comforts, for a

---

*As ever pedantry has its dangers. The author writes, "As for identifying 'ivory cradle,' I see that the image is more mysterious than I meant it to be. It was only meant to represent a crescent moon. However, I don't think what you wrote is contradictory, and I think you can leave it as it is unless you are bothered by it." Let the evidence stand!

coherence that will not go away. The endless search for that relieving and securing knowledge must seem without end. And yet it is life it-self, which "passeth all understanding." One hears still Hamlet's warn-ing, "There are more things in heaven and earth, Horatio, than are dreamt of in your philosophy." But given the patterns constituting the various orders of our lives, we seek to know their character and deter-mination—*why*, as a child might ask, are they so. And *why* does this happen, *why* that?

Poetry is not an explanation but a testament. Poetry is a company, a place to be which accommodates all and any. Its various melody is a life, passing—not a metaphor, or a description, just its literal acts of feeling, of finding, knowing the way. Implicitly the will to find such a way, to endure despite, to respond and secure with love the life one's been given, to provide for the sons one has borne, to make a place no matter where it can be—all these are particulars far beyond the reach of contesting attitudes or interpretation. In that sense it seems to me that these poems bear witness and carry forward the company which they have found. Why faith should at times seem to give such pain— one thinks of Francis ("Giovanni" was his given name) and Clare, Romeo and Juliet, as being almost one and the same persons in their star-crossed confusions—one must wonder. Isn't life itself the test if one is needed? Yet all the questions must still gather, the days and nights still flower, the story continue. So one follows such a music as this, moved by its determined integrity, relieved of all it so generously takes as burden of its own—wanting happiness too.

Part One

The Jesus of Cracow

The pigeon that brought us to Cracow groaned
outside our window, a pacing Jesus
with dirty feathers trying to get into
our room, his followers puffing their wings
behind him. There was a reason he lived
on that roof in all that shit, there was
a reason too for his horrible singing
in a register and rhythm somewhere
between sex and suffering so that
his small beak opened and closed on his one
aria; the others half-disowning
him—as they always did—so there was no
telling when there'd be a crowd of hundreds
smack in the middle of some square or just
a handful in hiding, hysterical
on a stone staircase where we saw them near
the ruined synagogue, 12 or 13
crazed birds huddled in that filth hoping we'd
go away. I liked how they hovered with
their wings half-opened, nervous as hell
and I quick took some pictures not noticing
there was an old woman inside
the open door, in the dark, not meaning
to scare her or intrude, and imagining
how she'd be a shadow in my picture,
a ghost behind the birds at the top
of the stairs, poor Mary of the shadows.
And I was sure I was right about Jesus—

but so was everyone—that we were blind
to the Kingdom, (John busy showing up
Peter, Peter always the last to get
things right). The bird was pacing even before
he woke from his deep sleep, he found himself
plodding across the roof urging those
sickening sounds from his throat. This time
he wanted to enter our hotel room,
we had to shut the window, he was a Jew
coming back for the Jews, doing penance,
as if he hadn't suffered enough.
I was only the mother of half-Jews
so I was guilty too, a Christian
hoping for forgiveness but not prepared
for his radical cries, his haunting moans.
The old man at the table collecting
a few cents for the empty synagogue
could have kicked the pigeon, cursed him, why not?
He knew every strung-out song too, and how
it came down to 109 Jews
in Cracow in 1999—the birds
avoiding the cemetery, its sparse grass,
its mutilated lion. There's no telling
what they would have said to one another,
I thought the rain was the time for it, the sky
ripping here, there, the sky a black cloth
puckered and blowing in the storm.
The pigeon hated rain, the dirt dripping
in his eyes; the old man lifted his face,
his white beard, and squinted at the clouds. I
knew my tears were ridiculous since I

never saved anyone or lost my whole
family, and there was no proof I wouldn't
turn my back if I had my chance, pressing
my head to my knees, gritting my teeth to
keep out the noise. The awful pigeon faced
the window, waved his cloaked arms, not a dove,
not an ounce of brilliance or peace, but a sky
so heavy it hurt, ready to open
in the next few hours and soak the city.

All Afternoon

That shame of staying in bed all afternoon
reading women's lives, trying to think like them.

I couldn't drink coffee or a glass of wine without
getting nervous, my exhaustion went back years,

it was a funnel drawing at my heart. Even my own
women wouldn't leave me alone, Nana's sister

praying to die at age 10, exchanging her life
for my grandmother's back in 1918, Italy,

she was just a girl, lecturing old men in the piazza,
asking: *What's this life worth?*

I left the shades drawn till the boys came from school,
dreading the phone, dreading neighbors

knocking at my door, waiting for the first crocus
like an upturned bell, for a grape hyacinth to raise

itself from the wet ground. It took all my effort
not to hate him. The room's light

was pink, nearly red through my blinds when the sun
came south around the house, my hand on my books,

and I was in Siena by then during the time of the plague
hearing death all around me, death from the street below

or in the wind entering my house for all I knew since
I never left my locked room, an invisible ring

around my finger, someone I never heard leaving a tray
of food by my door, fire through the high arched window,

a dove cooing, the three-year prayer
burning my mouth.

Airport Hotel

You had to see them in my light,
drones in matching shirts,
sellers of corn chips or tires, smoking
in the lobby and talking numbers
under artificial trees, and from where
I sat the jungle décor
and roar of planes outside
made their legs look like stumps,
a forest of khaki, a type
of laughter that could never
save the world. There was a television
above the bar, everyone wore
name plates pinned to their shirts
and I in my contempt made
a vow of non-forgiveness
and pulled on my aloof wings.
I was an angry bird and had my list
of grudges, which was long.
My son said, "You're a red
cardinal and I'm a nuthatch."
He was right that I might leave
a trail of small-time terror,
that there was something wrong
in my red breast and I
was soaked in my own blood,
that my singing pierced the air,

all my humility drained away
as I vowed to fight
forgiveness at all costs, and to keep
my wings moving.

Leaving Settefrati

I'm still trying to get the story straight—
stuck with the dead child, the one they left
in the ground when they left Italy for good, my grandmother,
her mother and brother heading down the mountain,
leaving the Town of Seven Brothers, the reddened roads
and waterless fountain, the war over. A day
like this 80 years ago—pulp sky, air like vinegar, the sun
a pale thumbprint—when no one dared look back
because of the ones watching, because of the dead girl,
the boy's twin who prayed to die.

They're gone now and I can't imitate
my grandmother's mounds of pasta that dried
like gold hair all over her kitchen since I wasn't
really watching but kept making her return to her dead sister.
Her sister maybe 10 when she died, who predicted
her own death months before the epidemic,
who, like a nun, sermoned old men
in the piazza till they laughed. Who said
she'd rather be with God and turned the war
against herself. Let's remember the ones

who want their deaths quiet and young,
knowing their limits. It's not enough for them
that trees return each year with their same
questions, pushing out from their fingertips, flowering green.
Think of the mother still grieving, sailing to America
in a stinking hole that caught fire one night

in the middle of the Atlantic and how she dragged
her two living children to the deck, knocking down
a sailor who blocked the stairs because she would not
go quietly. The dead girl had a different hunger

and could not stand the least violence. That final
August she told them: "I need to make the pilgrimage."
"Next year," said her mother. "That will be too late,
I'll be dead by then." Her mother must have swung
around in a kind of rage and terror. She must have almost
hit her but was trapped by the girl's stern face,
maybe a sickness, maybe a miracle, and so the child was allowed
to make the pilgrimage that night up the mountain and died
that fall in the flu epidemic, though it was her sister,
my grandmother, who was supposed to die,

who awoke from her fever to find the younger girl
turned to a pale shell, already dead beside her,
her aunt screaming. Her mother came back too late
from church and anyway forgot to bring the grapes
the child asked for. I found out the town's still not
on the map but hidden against a mountain,
the one road a thread into a small spool, the names
of the old men who still meet in the piazza
are the names of my childhood, Town of Umber,
though the faces are different, and their house

has fallen, though I drove the winding road,
Town of Waterwheel, and walked in their dust to see it,
and found someone who remembered them
and could say their names though what remained

was rubble and I was pregnant and hadn't eaten
and the one store was closed so I turned my back
even as I passed the stone trough she'd described
where she washed clothes, even as I looked over
the valley, holding my belly that was puffed out
like a pink moon, Town of Nether, another green

day, I'm there.

My Son and I See the Arms and Armor Exhibit

I don't want to cross to a world where the sky
is wet and cold and a knight rides from the woods

just as thaw is reversing. I don't want to pity his body
rubbed raw by armor that all day wore

the melted face of the sun, all night slept
empty beside him. My young son studies

swords and guns, asks me to read
what each is called: burnished shields,

rubied scabbards, lances, coats of mail.
The mounted knight with blue plume

that he likes so much rides home, bored
with crusading, bored with blood, restless

boredom of rapists, rusted weapons, and cadavers
in fields of mud who once threw themselves

like wind against trees, even oaks, even bulkheads,
thrashing like sea, like storm. Daggers,

crossbows, muskets. Iron and gold.
Worn also by boys, monks, and the girl Joan.

My son hangs tight to me, presses his free hand
to the glass. I lift him in my arms to see

the bodiless armor and its cavity, its hole
of questions: silver husk, like my own. I want to let it go,

done with my war, my failures,
my pitted shield and metallic smile,

sick of what endures with its humiliating
glare and polish, as if I could be something new,

washed of blood, ready to be pardoned
as I bring us out again onto the stone steps

and the city in its din of rain.

On the River

Small comfort: words written, not shouted.
Each frame of the day clear,
like the way the back of each boy's head
looked, the unclenched light on the river,
and the rafts with the roars of children.
From this the events of the afternoon, the facts,

rise from the rafts and float the way facts
do, becoming impermeable, like something shouted,
the water's sparks jumping, the water clear
down to slimy rocks sticking up as if they're heads
gray and silent, or jagged slabs in the river
catching the rubber boats, thrilling the children.

A day of parents with their boy children,
boy scouts scouting the Delaware not for facts
but for adventure, reckless and shouting.
I'm in the middle of the boat, not clear
about another parent who holds sway and thinks he heads
our raft, so intense about steering the river

he keeps whacking me with his paddle, the quiet river
his burden, the lazy bodies of the children
becoming more stubborn than facts.
It's not unusual for parents to be shouting
or for them to feel they'll never make things clear
but he grabs his son's neck holding his head

down in the muddy bottom of the raft, a small blond head
and cringing body, the raft grazing the river,
and a calm sharpens me as I look at each of the children,
a calm squaring my shoulders till I'm sure finally of certain facts,
so sure that I know he'll never hear me shouting
and it would only take one swing of my paddle to clear

his confusion. A few white blisters across an otherwise clear
sky, sweet blue, the boy raising himself, his head
bowed in the front of the raft, my son alongside him down the river,
and I wish I were as reckless as the children,
not needing to arrange my facts
or to knead my heart still from where it pumps, shouting

like the shouting swirls around the rocks in the river,
and the children, their clear
eyes steady as facts, the proud tilt of their upturned heads.

The Beekeeper's Sorrow

It's a white hunger that's dined on the hive.
Opening the house she finds ruin, moth
larvae hollowing the combs, tiny monsters
lolling in honey, their stubby, hairy bodies
everywhere. It happens to bees
weakened or sick who can't fight, can't consume
moth eggs quick enough. Flies hang around,
yellow jackets bombard the entrance,
and the handful of honey bees left alive
spiral off the hive heading out
for new territory. All day falling leaves pant
across the meadow where the small white house
is perched right in the open for
everyone to see. Will she put her hand in
to scrape the hive bare? Find
where there's still a corner of silky wax?
A house of love? Will she put her hand in?
The drones all sick or dead, curled
in the dark—and where is the queen?

American Music

Did you hear them when the bee truck overturned?

So many thousands of bees escaping like tiny striped convicts humming a song of freedom.

Who understands how important bees are? Just a few crazy people who put their hands right into the hives. These days machines imitate bees and drown them out, no one listens as they thread summer through its needle to capture the viscous sunlight, no one knows their fine language, the maps danced while they're drunk on perfume, fresh from licking the open mouths of flowers.

The day was hot and humid, the air so green and laden. The bees sang and swam, small American bees rising to the Gershwin Rhapsody. Local bee keepers who heard of the disaster arrived too late and stood like conductors without an orchestra, trying to speak with their hands. While all around poisoned bees dropped like rain or hail.

In the Parking Lot

The wisteria grown wild and high,
invading the pines with fake lace
and lavender beards, as if winter left
odd ice bangles, the whole

tree row wound with thick, muscled vines.
Were the trees encumbered? Did they like
sleeping in each other's arms? In the home

of the trees where flesh met flesh
and light came through the needles
and blew open the small petals, no one

would ever climb that high to separate trunk
and twisted arms. No one would kill
the purple hanging nests. In the home

of the trees I looked up to see
engorged breasts, ecstatic tongues,
an orgy in full sun, wind
singing, the drunken breath.

On the Hill

I was weeks away from giving birth when we talked
about your death, thinking there'd be time
to get me on my feet again after the baby came.

But in the month you lingered at St. Vincent's, I could
hardly get there. A friend held my baby downstairs
while I wandered corridors to find you changed,

fighting morphine to stay conscious, your legs blackened
to the waist, and in the week since I'd last seen you,
white veins of cancer strung across your eyes.

In the filthy bathroom off the lobby I nursed the baby,
hoping he'd hurry, scared of the dried blood
I'd seen smeared on your fingers, on your head,

scared of who might walk in while I leaned
against the wall of the cramped bathroom,
the baby frantic for my milk. Nothing was how

I wanted it to be, you swimming in your poisonous soup,
dying your crumb-by-crumb death.
Even now there's something I keep trying to say

that never comes out right, though we used to say
so much, sitting over tea, talking about God.
I kept your ashes two years in a ziplock bag.

The day I took the kids and left, I let loose
your ashes on the hill behind the house
and they spilled over moss and blue-gray rocks,

the powder of your diseased *corpus*
burning for us all, for our abiding failures.
Blessed are the ones who sing,

as you do, blessed are the bandages,
and the hands that wrap them. Blessed
are fire to change us, ice

to hold us fast, and the sound
the air makes swallowing our souls.

for Michael Pelonero, 1950–1992

The Same Dream

Why do you ask? He had the same dream
as anyone. He meant for her to be sure
so he stood each day at the corner
when she was due home from work
but never said a word to her. The old women
leaning out their windows didn't miss a thing,
they kept track, told her mother everything and then
some because the girl spoke English without
an accent, and because he was born here
and had been in the Navy—seasick three years.
It's just another love story about the stubbornness
love lives on as much as anything so when
her father started following him he'd leap off
the subway car at the last minute and leave
the old man waving his fist as the train pulled away.
And how the stubborn are slowly broken, be it money
or sickness. It wasn't betrayal in this case
since he was right about her and she was stronger
than all of them. Did it matter what he'd been physically—
doing handstands on the ship's guns—
if when he ran the candy store he gave half of it away?
He was ten years dead when she told me
she saw him in a dream. "I'm all right,"
he said, playing solitaire in a cloud like he did
all summer, never setting foot on our beach
but watching us through the picture window,
a deck of cards in his hands, or driving
from stand to stand looking for the best

tomatoes, holding and smelling them before
he'd put his money down, drying their seeds
on newspaper. The last time I saw him he stepped
out his door and stood on the steps waving at us,
the light over his head like a thousand birds around
his white hair and white shirt. He greeted her as though
it was 1925 and he'd finally—after weeks
of watching her—gotten the courage to speak,
though they'd long forgotten how they defied
her family and married right away. In the beginning
all he could say was he wanted her to be sure,
which she was. Her eyes half-closed, she told me
how they walked together for the first time one
evening after work looking for a place to eat,
the sky beet-red over the river, one window after
another, and how even that was new to her:
not rushing home, her mother throwing potatoes
if she came through the door five minutes late.
They looked in at white tablecloths and strangers eating
till the air felt so cold on their faces and legs
they ducked into the next restaurant, and by then
everything seemed long settled, settled before
he'd ever spoken to her, so that the moment
they sat down and faced each other across
the table something came alive, egglike
in her hand or her heart, small waking sounds
filling the space between them,
a rustling, a flickering in the smoky air.

Morning in Florence, San Marco

I was out the door and halfway to the elevator
when he threatened to throw
my clothes into the lobby. With the baby to think of
I had to know when to stay or go

so I headed out alone into the consoling brown light
off the river, feeling the child
swimming carefully inside me as I walked to see
Fra Angelico's frescoes in cells

where monks once slept and knelt, contemplated
and vanished; where in rapture he worked
fast as the plaster dried to get light to wash the wall
the way God would have done it.

At the top of the stairs the paint quickened:
it was Gabriel appearing to Mary
and it was seamless how he crossed worlds, an angel
with wings wide as a field

visible and more real than her wooden
three-legged stool or her blue robe
hiding her thin legs. Mary hugged her chest
as if to ward off a chill

or as if she felt her breasts already changing.
I held my hand beneath my belly

for relief from long corridors and tight
passion rooms. I walked cell to cell

carrying my airy satchel of the unknown, wishing for
a narrow bed and a day or week
of quiet, some place safe to wait with my secrets,
my terrifying news.

Geraniums

At the party I hear the true story of her death.
Afterwards I find a night so luminous, the moon's
slim cup in the bare spindles, and stars,
stark and flaring, the first mild night of the year.

Murdered, you say, her daughters
refusing her an IV of glucose and water when she passed out,
saying it was her wish, *but that's what
happens to alcoholics when they detox.*

You tried to rally her friends, her parish priest,
but couldn't save her. The morning you were set for court,
one last try, the call came: the old woman
dead of dehydration and the daughters' hatred.

Could it be enough that she squeezed your hand
from her blossom of oblivion? Wanting the kind
of beauty you knew about. Having the same
sad craving as the Chopin prelude you play

so easily at the party. This music
some can't live without. Still, it amazes me
that the daughters got away with it. For four days
the nurse played the tape of her favorite

hymn over and over against
the daughters' orders, organ music droning

in the walls while they scrawled
her obituary in the next room. It's like an opera,

but it's not, so many people moving
in and out of her room, nodding,
like this party, the new geraniums on the table,
their bitter smell, their quiet, red mouths.

She Died

Because it's different for the unmourned
she ended up kneeling near her bed,
her open eyes searching for the gash
in her blue room, saying her prayers
into the shameful stillness. Sometimes
the dead look like houses abandoned
without warning: my old grandmother's
slightly gaped mouth like a door half-open,
my brother's tight grimace—a drawer stuck,
forever crooked like that. But she
was a house rotting bit by bit with
its slow life burning in a back room,
and I can almost hear her alcohol-
slurred voice, her cigarette-hacking voice
as it sounded on the other end
of the phone, before I'd pass it to
my mother, and I think: God keep me
from such love and its bread of emptiness,
God keep me from the passive house of
splintered floorboards, I mean her body's
broken windows, curtains so filthy
bugs won't eat them, a house where a soul
has been lost so long no one thinks twice
about her, though finally she falls
on her knees and after awhile
someone notices she died.

My Brother with Shark

In this one from the time Daddy took you
shark hunting, you pose with your catch

on the boat prepped with giant hooks, gaffs, punctured
cans of chum, and the shark-man hired

to ensure you came home happy and with all
your body parts. Later Daddy complained

that it wasn't a sport to shoot the sharks,
but the stranger had jagged scars down his arm

to prove his point. The boat trolled slow
till one hit and they strapped

you in the fighting chair to work hours
tiring it, to reel it in and let it out,

the boat rocking with anger and joy
till finally the shark was alongside the hull still

wrestling the hook and the shark man clubbed and shot it
as if he thought it couldn't die.

After that Daddy knew who was more dangerous.
But from this picture I can't tell what you thought.

You're stooped in flagrant daylight, grinning at the camera,
both your hands pull up the shark's dead head,

its silver body splayed
across the boat-deck. The shark with its own

little grin, the huge, pink stomach it had
vomited hanging from its mouth

as if it had laughed itself
into a terrible state.

Packing

What you never saw: rodents in the walls
ragging the insulation; sacs
where moths slept and savored your books;
closets stale with dust and old clothes
like the baby sweaters you won't
disturb as if a cry might rush
through empty buttonholes.
Has the house taken on your fear?
Close to the day you're set to leave
sitting in the basement with a deranged
bag of toys to sort, you hear rain
turning torrential, dripping
from windows then a flood
of water down the walls,
running round your feet like a dream
you had of the house being
carried away, an act
of God you think, but you won't say so.

One Life

All over the island wild chickens zip
through tropical foliage; half the night roosters
swear and call for war. Once, my friend's cat
caught a just-hatched one. We watched her
chase the cat and pluck the bird from between its paws
before it could start its torture. Then with my son she set up

the chick hospital: heat-lamp, water, ground corn.
My friend's like that with animals, no matter that there's
all those rusty chickens along roadsides,
no matter the time it takes rescuing birds that hit
windows or huge toads that stare up at rain
from the middle of the road. Like that chick.

Even with useless wings it escaped the next night.
When the kids were asleep we heard it peeping
behind the oven. After that she kept it
in a big box near her canary for company.
I haven't mentioned the couple returning from China
who stopped there to rest between flights.

They had that stunned new-parent look
as they showed us the baby girl they'd adopted.
It's too hard to think what was done to her.
Her little wrists tied to the crib.
Worse still, what wasn't done. How at eight months
she weighed little more than my sons weighed at birth.

They arrived as we were leaving and the whole
way home on the plane I saw her tiny face,
the way it looked when she locked
her eyes into mine. I can't keep track
of these lives the way my friend does.
Weeks later she calls to say

she let the chick loose, he's one more
noisy rooster now hanging around
her flower farm. The canary misses him though,
misses him terribly and flies
wildly in its cage whenever somewhere outside
the cat has caught another chick.

Vermont Trees

Below birds crossing the lake of the sky
and purple martins on power lines, down
to the trees and one thing my brother said
that stays with me from Long Island to Vermont,
something about trees being conductors
of spirit, such bloody light they draw
toward themselves, toward us, into fields
and planted rows, like the old oak that looks
exhausted and smells of fire twisting through
its trunk and into its skirt of roots.
What it holds up, what it does for us,
we'll never know. Not while trucks speed past
white houses and a man biting a cigar
shoves suitcases into his trunk, never
looking up at the ropes in the sky,
never noticing who is drowning in air.
Who can fathom the steadfastness of trees,
or see them for what they are in their robes,
or get past our unspoken envy for the pure
light that changes them till they're speaking,
the wind coming up from below
to loosen their tongues, each one swaying:
honey locusts, willow, apple, the clefts
in their backs bearing up against rot,
their leaves deep green. Would anyone guess
that in these woods there were once trees
three people could link themselves around?
Old as that, so I feel, I'm sure I feel,

something missing when we hike across the farm
and into the forest. Some gaping loss singing sweetly,
too sweet, all around us while we climb,
out of breath and dizzy, some hole at my back
when we stop to catch the view—Vermont
to New York, we're that high—
mountain ranges stained violet and receding
into the horizon, and still there's no reconciling
that I'm an epidemic, scavenger, death threat,
even though I leave the apples on their branches
and try to step around the moss into this air heavy
with summer: late August when wind and blood
change direction and we head for
the final adornments, pine cones like bells,
whole mountainsides of them ringing
from their tall green steeples.

Eight Birds

I'll never be as ready
as that day when they landed
by my right hand, birds
zigzagging in surf then
hopping sideways toward me,
eight of them settling so close
I could have picked one up,

birds on one side, him on
the other; he was amazed that though
I talked and squirmed in my chair
the birds stayed ten minutes, maybe more.
I gripped a book with sunlit
fingers to keep my joy
to myself. Nothing mattered then

but the color of water against
the color of sky, those blues
touching, and the birds' black eyes
staring straight across
the waves. If I'd known how bad
it would get in the months to come I'd have
held onto what I saw that day,

teaching myself to hover above
my own body while I pressed
the broken lock on my bedroom door,
while he walked the house and yard

naked, coming up from behind me
as I read on the porch. I'd have tried
to remember those birds while I packed

in secret, my arms bird-strung, bent at
the elbows for sudden ascension, for climbing
air-shelves away from our house.
These days I'm carried by memory,
though who cares that he loved me,
that he once watched eight birds land
by my side, eight birds crouching

on stick legs in the hot sand,
making almost inaudible sounds
so I had to lean under the wind,
I had to close my eyes to hear them.

Fourth of July

When I drowned them in the sink—since all
fireworks were legal on that island

and he went out for a burger and came back
with enough fire power to start a small war—

it was my curse to be right and wrong at the same time,
his curse to have a mother who

could see bloody hands and hear screaming.
There was a meeting of flood and fire

where fire needs air and water needs
something to catch it, and who was there to hold

me back—righteous water—and who was there
to give him air, to explain that what he wanted was

shock after shock, his hands uncupping fire, so he
could turn to us and say *Behold the light,*

for he was the man among us and wanted to get down
on one knee and make his miracles.

Late afternoon, between storms, we shoved outrigger canoes
off sand and paddled onto waves that came

toward us like moving stairs. We watched for green
sea turtles, the sky bruised above

the mountains, the falling sun setting off scarlet streaks.
By dark we were back on the beach,

so crowded now we couldn't get near the water.
We were surrounded by a mass

of explosions, fire crackers by the hundreds stammered
in sand, the whir and simmer

of a thousand dying stars arcing over our heads.
Before long I could taste

the gun powder of my own spirit. Thank God
my friend let him play with a few fireworks.

I left them and carried home my youngest. I tried
to understand why we could not remain

one body—my first born, his brothers, and I—
why we had to spark and screech,

blowing apart like that.

Slope of Stone and Dirt

It wasn't the house I loved or later missed,
the house with its rotting foundations that seemed

so small when we climbed the hill,
like the winter morning my son and I looked back

to find it distant, padded with snow.
We turned then and rose onto rock ledge

almost tripping over a dead deer—heart the birds
came for, throat split, eyes open.

Not the house, but what sloped up from the back door:
green boulders, broken dogwood,

the pride-of-India that blew down the year after I left.
Not the rooms, which grew dank. Not

the floors I paced or what flew
down the halls. A house listens

then confesses everything. Pipes burst,
plaster buckles, mice scratch inside the walls where

some die and leave the bells of decay ringing, ringing.
Think of the fire in the kitchen

and how I stood—9 months pregnant—on a chair washing
black soot. Think of the end, someone

pounding doors, the malicious flights of stairs. The last time
I climbed my hill trying not to trample

the moss, I didn't know that what I'd miss was not the house
but the slope of stone and dirt, dead trees

fallen into beds of leaves, a half-gone paradise.
When I broke myself open

I could never go back. When I broke
I was an arrow in love with my life again: I was harsh,

stooped from the pain, enraged.

The Woods Behind the House

A *perfect day*, we said, three mothers.
Sane air with its shard light.
Behind the house a diversion of slim trees the boys
wandered through playing hide-and-seek till one
came screaming from the inner-sleeve,
the farther circle of dense brush. It was my son
who'd never before made such sounds of terror,
his shirt dotted with stunned
yellowjackets, welts
on his legs, throat, and chest. And how

could I think of death on a day like this?
Home from the hospital he rested with ice packs
while I got into bed. It was my own death
that seemed nearer now, not his:
nervous heart, babbling brook blood.
His younger brother beside me,
touching my hair. For now the pain was everywhere.
It moved through our roots, tree to tree,
a tree-shaped pain with its old, heady canopy,
its muscled trunk and a burrow below
where something rotten and hollow
was inner-lit and fiery
with crazed, yellow-streaked, heralds.

For That Moment

The sky was a hive throwing out yellow bees.
Only a few were angry and that was light
rubbing its wings, but mostly light fell as if
falling were rising, stripping the trees into
gold tatters like when I was a child and walked
around my block, in and out of light's patches,
or stared, in school, at an overflowing sky
that skimmed the dirty glass, my teacher so thin
light almost splintered her when she hoisted
the pole to close the windows. She taught us
self-pity, worrying me with her poverty,
her sick mother, insisting we pray together
though one boy refused to bow his head
when she called me up to recite the 23rd psalm,
mispronouncing my name that whole year.
Not that I'd walked that valley, only the same
few streets, but already felt I'd come
to the wrong place, stepping back far enough
to watch my lost self, which went on for years
till one midnight in New York City my husband
pulled the car to the curb and got out, taking the keys.
He came round to the passenger side and I locked
the door. He was already yelling, or just talking,
I can't remember, ordering me to apologize.
When a crowd of teenagers came from the park
and stood around the car jeering, a streetlamp
staring down at us, I knew I'd finally arrived
at the place I never wanted to go and I'd have

to turn around, and as if coming back to myself
begin walking toward this dirt road on which
the relentless light of October cracks the trees,
and the hills are radiant with decay, where the last
warmth hits my face and shoulders and someone
near me walks so fast he makes circles
around me, while I urge my stiff hip and turn
just so toward the ruptured clouds in the west.

Glory

Crows, dirty crows routing a hawk,
the swim and swoop of black
shriekers, thirty of them at least
and the hawk heading out.

They own everything now: trees
with their dresses torn. They stake out
the corners of my yard, at dawn
they land on my roof.

Along the railing one marches
toward my bird-feeder, fat flesh-eater
scaring the songbirds. One
rips at the garbage. To hell

with live-and-let-live. They're screaming
now in the woods, on the shoulders
of yellow weeping oaks. They fuck
their sisters. They eat their babies.

How come they're never dead
on the side of the road?
And what about the meek and lame?
And the glory of the innocent? What

about the thumb-sized heart-
broken birds? The ones who

die in their sleep, their long beaks
warm from probing flowers' throats

and answering the trumpets.
Their emerald bellies heave.
One last time they heave,
having worked their whole lives

to stay aloft.

Part Two

Ivory Cradle

The air smells of what's coming. Something
sweet and cold slows the trees. Though summer's lost
I still hear where hornets
made a paper nest on the porch—
the kids and I watching them pivot up
the small opening. Remember
how you asked if I was happy? The air ripped
near my ears like the hornets' sound,
their nest growing till we swept it
down one night then kept it the next morning
for its shape like a bit of clay
thrown by a small potter.

*

Slowly, since no one's touched me for, oh,
a hundred years or more, and I feel like an old fresco
swimming in dust, a naked woman
with a tender vine painted
over her genitals and breasts, who stayed
on that wall for years though her belly
swelled and her mouth was gaping.
When your hand rests on me I want
to fall apart, for once. Skin
wrinkling against the sudden chill of air,
all my parts shaken with cold.

*

I woke at peace, snow clutching the trees,
the woods startled white against
the sodden sky, that heaviness
over us and the world stopped
under its white vision. I drove
the night before through wild
snow against the windshield
and then slept my old sleep, exhausted finally,
not once waking in the dark. This morning
I thought how your voice was like snow
filling all these bare places, your eyes
full of grief that love could begin again,
even now, in this cold, with winter's
vacant light hanging over us.

*

The sky was full like the sea
of wandering phosphorous that came
with its old forgotten lives and swelled
closer though we hardly looked
and when we did it was the ivory cradle,
polished and rocking—so empty
over the trees—that caught our eyes
because it belonged to us; and I,
who never had the patience to find
patterns in stars but only stood
helpless, my feet digging in cold sand,
waiting, listening to the surf
rise and fall, lay down with you
for a better view, though no tunnel
opened up, no vision completed us,

even for a moment. But we were happy,
your hand with its heat and bones
just so around mine while we watched
the flowering dark.

                          *

In freezing rain I drove
the hundred miles to see you, no light,
though it was day, the sky was a mouth
biting a wad of cloth. Where the highway
split, a hawk was frozen on a pole, its wings
half-opened—two pinched fans—
it must have tried to save itself, too late
to shake off the ice, it stayed that way,
leaning on wind.
                    How close I've come
wearing the voice of sleep, backed
into a corner. I don't know why
I woke up, why I'm still here,
one hand steering, one on the radio.

This Is How You Start

A tourist among saints and madwomen, where you never
belonged, like your dead friend who lived alone
near the Bowery, light rising through his cracked floorboards,
and you giving away your coat, your gloves. Hand open:
this blistered crust, this dusty cup. Your face slapped
against the white flank of wind.
After so many false starts it comes to this:
that it no longer seems insane to court loss;
that you invite a certain looseness of mind talking all day
to statues, waiting for God to come
scratching and digging at the glitter of flesh.
What did you want? Bruised apples?
Rain playing the trees? Some music to soften
the world's blow? Something to rescue you
from safety, the illness that was your life?
It's good to be one of thousands out walking
the streets, each one hemmed in by that blank country.
It's good to think that the taxi is a raft, the street
a river, the driver a ferryman pushing off
from the wet curb then disappearing
just as you catch something in his look.
You could walk like this for days or years,
your loneliness burning itself out, burning itself
down like a candle to its blackened rim.
Sometimes all you want is to wake sobbing
in green light till you're so forgiven
you can't remember how things got this way,
till you're in the room you slept in as a child,

the one with the needlepoint prayer tacked above
the bed, someone in another corner
of the house whispering your name, folding
your clothes, till you're here again with this
crust of bread, this dusty water—so good
to hold these crumbs in your mouth, the sun
on the back of your neck as you mumble
some prayer, the whole mottled world swimming by.

Dialogue: 14th Century

Doesn't hope have doors and windows? Not blood like mucky sea water, not locked joints, a life prayer-stained and silent.

Underfoot the heartbeat of stones, overhead, the gray rain pawing the roof. Here, there are too many mice for one cat. My mouth feeds on dust and smell of mould.

Still, in utter darkness the great din sings in my ear.

Soon enough I'll be bone shale, with less than this bit of straw for warmth. Unable to hear the falling leaves scratching the walk. To see the moon's borrowed light cooling the trees. Will the cold still scrape then? Will the simple snow cross like an army to find me in my shallow bed? So painful such coming down, such rare whiteness hunched above the heavy, wet earth.

Do you believe in the clemency of words?

Do you keep your love in a pocket of your throat?

All these years I've known the only way out is to seal up the doors.

Let the bread rest in its wooden bowl . . . let the dried rose lose its red grip . . . let the darkness swallow our smiles and teeth, and the flecks of moonlight dress us.

Clare and Francis

Sister, you knew his thoughts as he thought them. You understood the circle of ashes and how he could only empty himself with prayer. He is not a bridge to the other world. He is not. He disappears the closer he gets to you. Standing before you he doesn't exist.

Sister, what smells more like him? The stench of a leper, or the wildflower growing off your muddy hut?

Where do you go at night when your body slumbers on the dirt floor? And the visions! Visions and voices! What comes together, this circle of sound and light passing like the ring around the autumn moon and you pregnant like the moon with this love, what comes together passing from him to you through the forested night?

Did you understand when you saw him as a child on the streets of Assisi? Did the sharp wool under your lush garments keep your mouth full of God?

These bodies shake off what you fear. Come meet him in the woods. The angels fall from trees, faint from hearing him speak like this. The simple dirt catches fire. Miles away a bright burning, the grove secreted by birds' songs overhead. If you hadn't been praying almost since your birth, wouldn't this love have killed you?

When he is ready, the word of God will write itself into his flesh. You will feel it. You can't help yourself that way. It will be as loud as life budding out of a cold, bare tree. God in your icy fingertips, God in the bird droppings, in the fog walking the hills, the pebbles under your feet. Sister Clare, this love gives the animals something to feed on. Just look at Francis, their plump, furry bodies taking up the flesh he throws off.

Augustine

How free is free anyway? Were the sheep free,
squalling babies that had to sleep

in their own shit, was that freedom? City
of flesh, its parts uncontrollable:

some nights he still dreams of her,
but what good is that?

Unmovable, because God picked
him up and didn't drop him to break like

so much glass; he'd been made for God
and he loved his own sin for making him himself,

though he would never mention her name or talk about
the son who died, that suffering

less than the bitterness of not being sure,
how that dogged him, and how he was no Jesus.

*

It becomes necessary to hate
a man like that, to bring God

back to shoulders, thighs, to the tea-stained
table. For the sake of love to want

the kingdom for the loved-one
even if it means self-exile, though a man

like that needs reason, needs
his burnt tongue, the thrill of repression.

Beauty in folds of skin only
sickens him.

*

But where is God if not here in the blue
fingernail? I don't mean

the sky with its back turned.
I mean here, God's drool

in my mouth. I mean the weight
of another, his smell so familiar,

the crooked tree with its white
peeling bark, or a tree

that becomes a shivering woman.
Why else was there singing or a hand

filling baskets with olives?
Why wait for forgiveness when

something like war will shatter fields,
torment houses? A little freedom,

just a measure of freedom in the mind
of a dying man

who would not focus on what tore
like hailstones at the roof,

who would not admit it was all
unfathomable and that his mind grew

tired or that his failures pulled at him
like small hooks. I'm no

opponent for him. What could I say,
choked as I am?

I can't get past my unknowing, which at times,
unexpectedly, brings me joy.

Clare Views the Body of Francis

When Francis of Assisi was dying
Clare was so ill she thought she'd die first and be there

to greet him when he came to the next world.
But it was Francis who kept her here, ordering her to eat

a bit of bread each day, to keep the taste of this world
on her tongue. I go back to this story over and over.

Clare starving herself. Francis dying.
And as if they were my own

I want Francis to live. Like watching you on the phone now,
the shape of your face changing for an instant

as it passes through you that your good friend
is dying, and you're helpless, thousands

of miles away. That's how I replayed
my brother's death for weeks, months,

as if it could be undone. How my parents
must have dreamed it, unable to close their eyes at night.

And I can't help wondering if Clare ever believed
she'd survive 30 years without Francis.

After he died the brothers carried him one last time
to San Damiano. They held him up

beneath the sister's window. There were sounds
from beyond, like scratching or yelping, light came

loose and swarmed his corpse.
The men watched in awe at how the women wept,

Clare radiant above his empty body.
That's how you rise now from your chair,

rise to your grief, your shining eyes on me,
your hand pressing mine so I'm stunned by what I'm losing,

what I've lost, stunned by how we go on, still loving
and loved, standing here, consumed by light.

Reading About the Earthquakes in Assisi

My first thought was of frescoes falling into piles
of blue and gold, Francis

broken again, his face creasing, knees buckling, his eyes
smarting from the precious dust;

and I pictured mounds of rubble along hillsides, collapsed houses
like my grandmother's in Italy

when I went there after her death, not expecting I'd find
the place in ruins; little left but

the remnant of a staircase she used to climb. I couldn't bring myself
to touch it or even snap a picture,

as if what was sacred had become ridiculous, Francis taking off
his clothes in the square,

renouncing his father, or the way my grandmother died, smelling
    at the end
of a sweet rot as she swam past

each threshold, the family hovering above her pretending she was
getting well, someone applying makeup

to her face while her last cries circled her bedroom.
Not till I saw her caved-in house

did I understand she was gone, she was no more
than the sounds a soul makes

working itself free. I was pregnant then, and wanted something
from her dead mouth,

from the others too who'd lived there and I thought of how Francis
got started, how he heard

that voice say three times: *Francis, repair my house,*
and him behaving as if stone walls

were no different than souls, going from one to the other,
and now, centuries later, the basilica swaying,

the ceiling falling on the friars, Francis with so much left to do,
covered in mortar, dirt,

his hands bleeding while overhead birds go wild.
Of course he understands about

starting over, he accepts his gorgeous loss, the holes that love made
in his body. But I have no certainty, none at all,

and it sickens me to see this, birds falling at his feet
the way that sparrow flew against

my back door the morning she died, I can't keep up with it all,
it's a bad joke all this rebuilding. I can't

lift the stones he hands me, what should I do with them?
I can't climb that staircase leading nowhere,

rising from debris.

Saints, Marriage, Desire

Catherine was the one who didn't eat for nine years,
didn't sleep more than an hour a day, I knew of her
from the book of extreme lives, stories I read
again and again, their mouths still moving,
their emaciated bodies, those enormous inner feasts
as if a soul could gnaw its own bones.
Women tuned to a life alone, not
alone so much as turned away
to face a bridegroom of their own making.
Catherine refused to marry though it was years
before her father finally relented
when he saw who like a dove hovered
above her head. And when disfigured by disease
what relief to have beauty behind her
so she could get on with advising the Pope,
healing the sick, prayers flinging her abandoned body.

*

When I had two children and a bad marriage I still
looked at infants and desired another child like a rung
on a blue ladder. The only way I knew to leave
the body. In the last hours of labor looking out
from the other side at the people in the room,
what did they know? The silvery child with my blood
like rosettes on his temple was my ride home.
The pain took me to the ledge and back
but I couldn't step through like Catherine
or even Clare who left her father's house
through the door of the dead to meet Francis.

Under spidery trees he sheared her gold hair
so when her male relatives rode furiously
to the monastery to find her, and saw she was useless
to them, shorn like that, they turned and went home.

*

Coming home from court
all I wanted was sleep, looking for escape
like times in the car when he yelled for so long
I wanted to open the door and fall out
just to get away. I couldn't welcome my pain
which was a narrow pain, not the wide
suffering asked for by the saints.
And though I waited for the bludgeon of light,
it didn't come. Even Teresa, who never went in
for mortifications of the body like Catherine or Clare
was one day knocked to the ground by her visions,
God's wide hand erasing her past so this grandchild of a Jew
could write alone in her cell, scrutinized by the Inquisition,
listening to wind in the shutter slats, the raven sky
uncupping the stars till her wracked
body grew diaphanous, unmoored.

*

Often, I wondered who I'd be when it was over.
My sons coming and going, moving me with their questions.
I saw my failures on their faces. Not that I wanted to be
some starved saint collapsing, years dead
but dragged inward through room after room
as she closed each door of her body. Not that
I wanted to leave this life. I wanted to ride out
the loneliness of love. To remember
so fully, that memory is wiped clean, making space

in my body like the inside of a bell
so that one morning I'd rise—resonant, empty—
and stand by the window hearing light
seep into me, and the screeching of the birds.

Tiny Saviors

For G. S.

Speaking of devotion, my favorite was Dante in
Vita Nuova—the eagle with the heart in its mouth;

or the time I stood hours to see that Vermeer show,
the one where his paintings were together again after

hundreds of years and tiny saviors
rode motes of light through the window and into

the woman's eyes, the room
milky as the pearls around her neck. When we met

you didn't mind my wound like a small
flame, my bruised aura. You said your whole life

changed, your familiar things illumined:
books of dust, the velvet chair with its claw feet,

the street lamp's mottled shards across the floor
of your walk-up where I stood one night half-dressed

in the unholy neon, the only color in the room
from orchids, yellow and purple in the dark

contrasting my white pond flesh, my polite losses.
Why would you love *me*?

How crazy it seems when we stand in front
of your speckled mirror, or when I drive home to my kids

watching you recede. Think of the Vermeers
separated after their brief reunion, shipped off

in crates to different parts of the world
though I wept that day surrounded by them.

And the radiance that began in the artist's window or his eye,
that began God knows where and found me in that room—

tell me, where is it now?

Palm Sunday, Mexico

Then why don't you come, with your tree, your tower,
why don't you speak? What's that humming
that bee sawing the air? At any moment it can be over,
this fist of happiness—some truck careening out of control,
some visitor inside the lungs, probing the brain. There's no
figure weaving through the garden. Through the lilies
and yellow iris, trampling the sweet alyssum
that grows in the rock cracks. The passion tree
is purple again. There's no one leaning into its flowers,
no one smeared with color. Instead it's the same story,
even if someone travels through mountain ranges and forests,
hardly able to breathe through a filthy city, unable to
strip away what writes her, alone again, into a new landscape
where she sits with her head in her arms from the vertigo.
There's no one dipping a hand into the fountain where
orange wasps drag their legs above the water,
no one laughing at her sitting on the hot stone
with her guards the dogs and sparrows hidden
in the bushes. Maybe suffering isn't personal.
Maybe it hardly matters except to wade through it,
the way she left him, left others too with just a vague idea
that love is possible, if not love then at least some peace.
Outside the walls it's holy week
and everything is for sale. Inside, how much
has been gained looking for you?

Mexico

Brown like the flank of a horse through the windshield,
an American driving for hours, he had almost made it.
No light, maybe a piece of moon and stars,
it happened so fast, the way things do sometimes,
someone crosses the line in an instant
and a decision to change, change her life,
the way I loved you suddenly, the way I turned to you
and though everyone was watching, you held
my face between your hands as if breaking a spell.
The American with his own innocence of death
and the darkness of the mountain road.
A car swerved in front of him and from its tail lights
swam five horses heading his way. How
something surreal was true: five horses
he drove into, an eye riding the windshield full
of terror, the car crushed, two horses dead.
But he was saved, after everything, after
the screams and blood, after his death in
a foreign land rose and fell away, and a violent love
lay across his body, he was saved.

The Room

The weight of the dirt beneath their fingernails,
the burden of their footsteps approaching my door,

so little time alone I sometimes wanted a sealed room
like the woman who lived inside the walls

of a church and through the stone squint
heard the world whispering. Days I went

without speaking when the children were away
and made a wall of books around my bed, even kept out

the light, which was nothing compared to her life alone
though someone kneaded her bread,

picked the pocked fruit by her door
or brought honey and tiny nuts

forever patient in their shells . . .
It's something to find the mother everywhere,

to be fed, while rotting pods
fell from wet trees and childlike questions

kept coming multitudinous from their sulfury eggs.
As if we are none of us orphans,

as if my efforts didn't always feel like failure
and my God was not a mother.

In the end the room felt too small though the walls
changed color like clouds

and anyway I found myself averting my eyes
never seeing what she saw: woody thorns,

copious blood. It's not that I had no use for suffering,
but in the end the room itself

was a burden. It was a question of which way to turn
and where the light came from.

I thought of windows and the grasping of summer.
The wind was purple by then and the children and I

ventured toward the water, dragging our things.
It was a question of how to live with anger.

I saw it for a moment when they waded into the shallow bay
and bent over all at once to see some crab or fish,

their backs in white glare. The room
was gone by then, or else so enormous

I couldn't see how we were held.
The sky was pale, quiet, as if calling us with its smallest

voice, as if the sky were a visitor,
approaching, backing off, blue hands waving,

a visitor I stopped and called after,
wherever I was, at least once or twice a day.

Que Será

On one side of the death mask birds sing
so loud, and the drums that beat beyond
the brick walls of the garden play a march
with trumpets and flutes, and the trees—
eucalyptus, hairy pines—are skeletons
almost filled in, almost fleshy.
And though the mask is black and smiling
and its teeth are horns, for once it's not
frightening, you just nod: *of course, of course*.
There's not much to it. You should worry more
about what comes after, not a few days
of pain, of passing, he said; someone else said
it's like giving birth, in and out
of the body, in and out. Hummingbirds
work the orange bulbous flowers now,
so fast, they won't have time for morphine, so
nervous, they won't notice the transition:
when dogs all bark in chorus and the wind
stops, and on bent stems the bright eyes
of the lilies stare right through you.

Hunger Garden

You'd think these plants are starved the way
the sun spills over the walls and glazes them,
the birds complaining, lilies burning,

and that the century plant is too proud
climbing toward its last bloom, an egret
turned to stone gazing into the clouds.

I can smell their hunger, what it would take
to fill them, more than rain for the bulging
avocados, more than light, its singed bees

settling in purple cups, the flowers bleating
like lambs. Such awful hunger runs in the stems'
juice till something final snaps their necks,

a shadow of crushed berries falling around
the roots. All afternoon light's opposite
rises up tree trunks, submerging the garden,

the hollows fill with wing-beats of gnats.
You can find me in the tent of open
mouths, darling, where it's growing late. No one

else hears what I hear, the roses' pink shame,
the rasp of iris. When the sky's
its deepest blue the mouths will rest,

the wind will fall on its knees. Lover of
my hunger, I cannot help how my hand
reaches to soothe them, picking the dead blooms.

I let them brush against my hair while I
wait on the cracked cement bench, listening
to their labored breathing.

Parable

The parable of the pears was the one never repeated
because it had to do with sex, and more than sex
it was Jesus at his best showing them secrets
about the different kinds of love. There was a pear
whose brown skin had the whole rough hillside in it,
but inside so sweet he had to lie down to eat it,
and a more rare, red-skinned pear. It had no shame.
The harsh Jesus of the figs and vines
was undone, thankful, he was brimming,
in his mouth that taste he could never confide,
they would never believe him, they still wore
the dullness, they still thought day to day,
something simple might change their lives if only
they listened, if only they forgot everything
they knew, something of heaven would sprout
from their mouths if only they were ready for its flavor.

Between Heaven and Earth

Not from philosophers or tarot cards or from a stringy-haired
woman caressing my palm. I who tore apart

cloud after cloud looking for a sign. Who practiced Bach
with stiff fingers trying to hear, and dug

in riverbeds and peatbogs, and walked and walked
and counted hundreds of thousands

of severed hands and gouged-out eyes. In the woods I found
an abandoned nest and peeled half the shell

off an egg, making a cradle. Inside a chick lay curled
in the position of hope, with a blotch of blood

on its belly, its head tucked, its speck of a beak
pointing at its heart. Give me a hint, just

a word to suck on, I'm so hungry and this
is taking so long. I refuse to renounce a damn thing.

I refuse to take it on the chin again or to adjust my methods:
I leave cataloguing to people who need

to keep busy, let them play with fragments
of parchment trying to match dust to dust. I stay off ladders.

I go after the TV with a shotgun
and bury it without prayers because when the time comes

it's the radio that will surprise us
with its access to other worlds and then the sense of smell

will finally return, as it was eons ago,
and the odor of milk, sweet and sticky, blue

and reflective in its puddles on the floor from a mother's sobbing
because she knows everything

is whole and broken at the same time which is why
they want to drug her the moment

her vision is most clear and her pain the worst,
when she's bearing down, crossing the boundary,

they want her to behave, they hate screaming
and her body arching like that. Always, a world

between worlds. Something holding me down like his leg
hooked over my hip, two passengers on the torn

sheet, the hissing of pipes all night
to accompany us. The sky moves through the window

and the cold, more and more, wears me out, making me
take up my fear the way some women take up knitting—

though I believe in the near-death of snow
and all it buries, even if trees are laughing at me,

their bare fingers pointing up,
even if the dead are walking on us, talking behind our backs,

and the pond is frozen and animals inert in their burrows.
When it comes down, heavy and white,

I want to stand inside its sadness. The snow
won't speak of where it came from. Though I'm listening,

my ear pressed against wind,
trying to catch the very moment it passes into this world.

Needle and Thread

There was something childlike about the clinging limbs
finding their places in the dark bed; or plantlike, vines
sewing themselves together, a needle and thread
made of skin and hair, sewing, sewing, made of breath.
How many lives could go on at once,
superimposed, as when he dreamed and she dreamed
and the green light of the clock kept changing or the stars
kept pulsing—the sex of stars—and she half
woke up and listened for him to see
if he were sleeping and then slipped back
into the stickiness of that other world she could never
wash off, her dreams making fun of her earnest life
and all the death she was trying to escape each night.
In the bed they moved close, then apart, then close again,
night a wall falling on them, one hated the dark,
one loved it, a wall pressing them together, a moist
mortar where skin met skin and penetrated each
in a different way so that he turned toward her
and she wondered if it was innocence
or foolishness that kept her always surprised, throwing
her head back and gasping.

Yankees

For beauty, the men came toward us across the field,
and when they stood trance-still, or when they backed
hard against the wall, it seemed part of some
greater design, or when one swung, twisting
his torso and bending his knees at the same time
as the ball flew and the crowd erupted,
I was in thrall to all of them, because they held back
then hit for their lives, because one gently lifted
his arm to meet the ball as if his own child
were falling toward him through thin air.
I even laughed at the men throwing beer
which drizzled onto my hair, and the one
yelling obscenities at the other team.
The blinding lights helped me see
their perfection, and I became a devotee—
not just for the sake of my sons, my arms around them—
though it was strange to be a woman then,
to love them that much, the arena
filled with men who were ready and had chosen
their weapons, so when the ball disappeared
for the last time all of us screamed
and rose from our seats so grateful
for our own violence which got us
this far without torture or mutilation,
and to one team brought to their knees,
and to the heroes, small in the distance,
holding each other, rejoicing.

I Can Be Bread

It was him with his fear of swords.
It was him with his cold skin,
his sunken eyes, his crooked smile,
his love of honey, anything
sweet, really. Anything fragrant.
Who else but the celibate could show
the way. It was him naked,
frail, his body worn, eaten by pain,
his body ecstatic, its thick
hairs holding the light.
Him with his arms out, his eyes
oozing, the light killing him.
Him with his puckered penis,
his bare feet in the cold
stream where he relieves himself,
o lion barking back. O
bloody hand on my breast.
The light has many names,
many dreams, he steps farther
into the water. Light
side-stabs him. I offer my mouth.
I offer my spread legs. I
can appear or disappear
in the water. I can torture
him with honey. I can be
bread. I can kneel. I can
carry my own bed. The light
has many names. I can

be naked, unafraid. I can be
in the same stream or I can
walk away, a lion
barking back, squatting, dripping
my bloody wine, bearing
up in that light,
bearing the light.

Bohemia

We heard the river, beyond that, hammering.
You leaned out the window and spread your arms

above rocks and across from the castle
saying you wanted to fly (my bird) some urge

pulling you in a country once big on defenestration
and other gory political endings.

I grabbed your shirt, lace curtains in my face.
Even when we crossed the bridge into the square,

even when we sat on rickety benches and watched
the clouds' next epoch—the sky wounded, light erased—

I felt it too, wanting to leap some
hurdle like the boy who clowned on the rail

above the amber river, or the bells sailing forward each hour.
I wanted to turn from my life: *Dear children,*

if only you could see this, love, love, Mom. Let danger
swing wide our window and let me stretch way out, yelling,

my knees pressed against the ledge.
Let's jump once more onto the escalator that hurled us at
    great speeds

far underground where we rode trains
trying to pronounce the names of stops. Or a bus going anywhere.

Think of a seed-pod exploding from a tree and you rising from sleep
to walk off a leg cramp, all the windows open

and the air wet over us. Because I never know
what's coming and I can't pray or beg anymore, I just tilt

my head toward my blind spot. Our last night
you limped back to bed beside me and sang the name

Cesky Krumlov in my ear. I slept
till workers began their banging and the sun

dropped heavy onto our legs.

Anne Marie Macari grew up in Queens, New York.
She is a graduate of Oberlin College and the
Sarah Lawrence College MFA program.
Her poems have previously appeared in journals such as
Field, Triquarterly, *and* The Ohio Review, *as well*
as in the anthology Models of the Universe, *published*
by Oberlin College Press. She lives in Lambertville, New Jersey,
with her three children.

CPSIA information can be obtained at www.ICGtesting.com
Printed in the USA
LVOW06s2305220915

455210LV00001B/6/P